ADVENTURES IN WHOLESALING

REAL ESTATE

Let Me Show You How

SHAUN YOUNG

Legal Disclaimer

Every effort has been made to accurately represent this product and it's potential. Even though this industry is one of the few where one can write their own check in terms of earnings, there is no guarantee that you will earn any money using the techniques and or ideas found in this book.

Examples in this book are not to be interpreted as a promise or guarantee of earnings. Earning potential is entirely dependent on the person applying the ideas and techniques that are contained in this book. The author does not purport this as a "get rich scheme." It will take hard work and dedication.

Your level of success in attaining the results possible in this book depends on the time you devote to your own success, your finances, knowledge and various applicable skills. Since these factors differ according to individuals, the author cannot guarantee your success or income level. Nor is the author responsible for any of your actions; you are. Concepts in this book may contain information that includes or is based upon forward-looking statements within the meaning of the securities litigation reform act of 1995. Forward-looking statements give expectations or forecasts of future events. You can identify these statements by the fact that they do not relate strictly to historical or current facts. They use words such as "anticipate," "estimate," "expect," "project," "intend," "plan," "believe," and other words and terms of similar meaning in connection with a description of potential earnings or financial performance. Any and all forward looking statements potentially contained in this book are intended to express the author's opinion of earnings potential. Many factors will be important in determining your actual results and no guarantees are made that you will achieve results similar to the author's or anybody else's, in fact no guarantees are made that you will achieve any results from the idea and techniques found in this book. The author is not an attorney if you need legal advice please seek an attorney.

Contents

Chapter 1

Mindset and Your WHY

Let me tell you something; If you don't have the right mindset going into wholesaling or any other business for that matter then don't do it! It's extremely important that before you approach our business that you get your mind right. Work on yourself first! I know that may sound like a cliché and everyone says it, work on you 1st, but it is absolutely 100% true. Success is 80% mental and 20% mechanics; meaning your mind is controlling everything so if you don't think you can do something you are right just as if you think you can do something you are also right. This business will try you. It will push you to your limits. It will also help you grow as an individual, but if you're not in the right mindset, you won't have the fortitude to stick with it. So let's discuss mindset a little bit more and ensure you get started with the proper one. Self-belief and determination is crucial to your success, and it cannot be pushed to the side. You have to believe in yourself. Make a promise to yourself right now to start living your best life. If you want to live an abundant life then you must start by having an abundance mindset. Do not allow defeating self-talk to take over your subconscious mind; I'm not saying it's easy and doesn't take work and effort but you must replace self-defeating talk with positive self-talk and action. Opportunities will be presented and created based on your actions and constant action will allow you to be better prepared for opportunities. Make goals that are realistic and attainable but think big. Do not limit yourself to the realm of comfortability. In order to grow you must push yourself beyond limits that are comfortable for you currently. The simple factor that separates those who fail from those who succeed is simply that those who will succeed chose to not quite on themselves. Everyone in this world is self-made however only the successful will admit it. Become successful by taking your destiny in your hands. We are no longer in the era of depending on a job that would pay you a retirement after 20 or 30 years; no those days are long gone. The sooner you realize that your future and destiny is in your hands the sooner you will take the serious action that it takes to change your circumstances. Of course life happens and life is happening to all of us all the time; but what does that mean to you? Does it mean that life is so hard or tough and challenging for you that you have to settle with being a victim of life? NO! It means that in spite of any circumstance life places before you; you will not let it defeat you. You and only you have the ability to turn something into an excuse or you can turn that very same thing into motivation. Use it to motivate you; use it for your fuel! I don't care if you have experienced great success in real estate investing or another business or you are flat broke this book will have something for all of you. Success and excuses cannot occupy the same space so therefore you must eliminate them. Rock bottom has always been a solid foundation to build upon; so even if you are one who feels you do not have the money that it takes to get started; you are wrong. You have to have the desire to succeed coupled with action; taking one step at a time towards your goals. You want to create daily routines to start your day that includes a wake up time, drink a glass of water, exercise of some sort for a minimum of 20-30 minutes to get the blood flowing, read positive literature or uplifting audio for at least a 20 minute period, now hit your schedule that you should have set for yourself before bed the previous day. Do this day in and day out. Develop good habits for yourself in order to eliminate some of your bad ones. How you do anything will be how you do everything; remember that!

Your Why...

Your Why is your driving force it's your driving factor it's what will keep you going; it's your fuel so to speak, and if you don't have a good source of fuel your fire won't burn very bright or very long. So here's a tip you can you to develop your why

This is a technique that one of my mentors shared with me to help develop a strong sense of Why and now I want to share it with you!

Take a blank sheet of paper and number it 1-7 giving each number is own line.

On line 1 WHY do you want to accomplish this

On line 2 WHY do you want to accomplish the line above

On line 3 WHY do you want to accomplish the line above

On line 4 WHY do you want to accomplish the line above

On line 5 WHY do you want to accomplish the line above

On line 6 WHY do you want to accomplish the line above

On line 7 WHY do you want to accomplish the line above

I want you to go 7 layers deep with the above exercise. Once you do this you will have a clear understanding of your Why. Write these down and refer to them often throughout the day especially when times get challenging. Developing a Why will be a key component for your success. Leave yourself no options to fail.

Chapter 2

Introduction to Wholesaling Concepts and Terms

First off I want to say thank you to all of my coaches and mentors as all of the concepts I will discuss in this book are methods and practices that I have learned from others that have come before me. Thanks Marvin, Gavin, Joe, Tom, Darryl etc etc.

Wholesaling in a nutshell is just finding a product at a discounted price so that you can sell at a discount price. In our case, it's finding a property at a discounted price, getting that property under contract, finding a cash buyer to match that contract to and selling that contract to that cash buyer. So you're essentially selling paper. You're getting houses under contract and you're selling that piece of paper; which is the agreement between you and that seller to your end buyer. So, to sum it up when you put a house under contract that gives you what's called equitable interest in the property and the right to market and sell your contract to an end buyer for profit. That's wholesaling real estate in a nutshell. Guys, it is not complicated, I don't want to overcomplicate this. Wholesaling real estate is nothing more than buying really low and selling low.

I would suggest starting locally. My suggestion if you want success is to start within your local market. Now, if you live in a town or a city that has a thousand people there, definitely try to find the next nearest big city that's nearby. Determining your market is, is super important because if you don't start off with the right market, you could discourage yourself and make yourself think this is a lot harder than it actually is. So my suggestion is your local market, then move to the next nearest big city that has at least 200 to 250,000 people. Now if you've got connections in other states, and I call those boots on the ground, then by all means utilize those boots on the ground. But if you don't have any of that and it's just you pick then your market based upon where you're located.

When it comes to picking what types of lists to use to market to motivated sellers I usually try to stack my lists, I try to combine things like maybe a distressed property code violations, tax lien and vacant. What I mean when I say vacant is no one's living in the property. It's just sitting there boarded up windows. Potentially grass has grown out of control, there is mail sticking out the mailbox etc. I mean, those are some great indications that that property is vacant. And think about it from this perspective, guys. If you owned a property and it was just sitting there vacant but you were still responsible for taxes, wouldn't you have some sort of a motivation to either make that property not be vacant or sell it? That's why we go after vacant properties. I stack that vacant list against code violations, tax liens, and probates.

What is a probate? A probate is a lead where someone has inherited a home. Johnlives in California. His grandmother unfortunately passed away in Kentucky. He doesn'twant to go to Kentucky; he doesn't want to see the house because of sentimental issues. He wants to get rid of it right away. Those are probate leads and those are awesome for us as well.

Chapter 3

7 Basic Steps in Real Estate Wholesaling

These aren't the official steps but these are 7 steps that I've put together to help you have a clear path to follow.

Step 1. Finding motivated sellers

Step 2. Evaluating the property/Getting the property under contract

Step 3. Marketing contract to cash buyers

Step 4. Assigning contract to buyer

Step 5. Sending documents to closing attorney or title company

Step 6. Closing the deal and collecting your assignment fee

Step 7. Prepare to do it all over again

First off I do not want to mislead you and have you believe things like you can get into real estate and become a millionaire with no money and none of your own credit. Now the previous statement could be true for a few but I want you to understand that you will need some funds to get started, even if it's simply gas money to drive around looking for properties to get under contract. Folks our business is all about marketing so either you figure out how to get marketing done for free or you prepare to have a consistent budget for it. Have you ever come across one of those infomercials on YouTube or Facebook that have a real estate guru saying something along the lines of "just a few short years ago I was dead broke living out of a car with my family eating from garbage cans when I discovered wholesaling real estate and then just like that my whole life changed overnight and yours can to; all you have to do is buy my course that I've created for $20,000 and you too can find success in real estate investing without using any of your own money or credit just like I did." Huh? How would this model work for the masses? It won't that's how. No, it does not take a ton of money but you want to have at least $500-$1000 to seriously get started but that doesn't mean you can't get started with only $100. There are plenty of free online sources to find basic information like YouTube for instance where I have my channel called "Adventures In Wholesaling". If you are reading the Ebook version the link to that channel is: https://www.youtube.com/channel/UCW1pZ9vQL7dk7GnLLf d18ww My channel and others give out a ton of free information. So it can be done using the aforementioned methods but if you want to shorten the learning curve and save yourself some stress then my suggestion is to find a

coach that you can connect with that has a one on one coaching program that you feel is worth your hard earned money. If you want my coaching services you can visit my online virtual course at:
www.adventuresinwholesaling.com

The way that I look at it is you will end up paying for your business one way or another; either through failed attempts at getting it right or on education and guidance right from the start so that you limit mistakes.

Below are a few basic terms that you will come across in your Adventures In Real Estate Wholesaling.

- ARV – After Repair Value

- MAO – Maximum Allowable Offer

- CRM – Customer Relationship Management

- RGA – Revenue Generating Activities

ARV – After Repair Value – A Key Assessment

Once you've located a potential property, successful wholesaling begins with your analysis of three numbers key to your success:

- Your purchase price

- A realistic cost to rehab and make it move-in ready

- The after-repair value (**ARV**)

Begin your assessment with the last one first. The **ARV** determines if it's worth continuing with this property or not.

The **ARV** is the market value for this property after it is rehabbed, beautiful, and move-in ready. This means defects cured, fully updated, new neutral paint on the walls, landscaping done, and real estate agents happily showing it to interested, prospective homebuyers.

The **ARV** determines what purchase price you can offer and still cover everything – the rehab expense, the selling costs, your profit, and the investor's profit. Learning this evaluation is a skill and a tool for all real estate investing. When this property is fully prepped and finally sold to a home buyer, that price should come in near or above your assessment of the **ARV**. Knowing the **ARV** is an organized process. It is an art as well as a science. Following the steps below will allow you to have a good handle on an **ARV** that you can document to show investors that this is a deal they can make a good profit on as well.

First, know the neighborhood and the section of town.

- What kind of home buyers are buying in this area? Come up with a general profile of the average buyer including income, age range, employers, children, etc.

- What is the typical listing description sold most often in this neighborhood? Make a profile of the average house including the square footage, number of bedrooms and bathrooms, lot size, extra rooms, etc.

- How close are schools, groceries, shopping, and employers?

- Gather the answers to all of the questions that homebuyers in this neighborhood care most about such as easy access to major thoroughfares, modern floor plans, etc.

Find and assess comparables.

This is much the same as it would be for any move-in ready house on the market.

- Assume your candidate property is fixed and ready to sell, and look for properties in the neighborhood that have closed in the last six months or less that are as similar in type as possible.

- If you can't find an exact match, take into account which sales have factors that you need to take into account as keeping the price a bit low or a bit high – for example, corner lots and other location variables, square footage, number of rooms, bedrooms and baths, and so on.

- The more closely your candidate property matches the profile of the average sale over the last several months, the better the market for it and the better you can work up an **ARV**.

Your determination of the **ARV** is not based on knowing the rehab or other costs. Instead, the types of factors that are listed on Zillow or Trulia are key – square footage, number of rooms, number of bedrooms and baths, style of house, updated kitchen and baths, modern open floor plan, yard, garage or parking situation, size of lot, neighborhood, extras such as landscaping or window coverings, and so on.

The **ARV** is not the price you will be asking from your sale to the real estate investor. It is the price the investor can sell it to the home buyer who will be moving into the property after the investor has brought it to top-of-market move-in ready condition.

You're preparing an attractive profit package for the investor! The **ARV** is the golden figure you will use to demonstrate to potential real estate investor-buyers that this is a great deal for them – so they should lock it in, fast!

ARV for rental investors

Rental investors typically can pay more than investors who intend to fix and flip. They don't spend as much fixing the house because it doesn't have to meet the same standard as sale houses. And, they are looking at a much longer time horizon than the flipper who needs to sell and make his profit now. The rental investor wants ongoing cash flow in the form of rent payments and is waiting for a potentially bigger profit on a sale years later.

Certain types of properties are ideal for rental investors, especially smaller houses (three bedroom/two bath) that don't need as much work. Home buyers pay less for such houses because they are small for the neighborhood, but to a rental investor, they will offer a nice return for years.

The rental **ARV** is based on comparables showing what similar houses bring in monthly for rent. Rental investors typically look at purchase values according to a formula based on monthly rentals using a factor of eight times the annual rental amount:

Monthly Rent x 12 = Annual Rent

Example: $1,000 x 12 = $12,000 Annual Rental Income

Annual Rental x 8 = Purchase Value

$12,000 x 8 = $96,000 Purchase by Rental Investor

This is the **gross rent multiplier** and is one of the biggest factors in determining if a rental property will be profitable for the investor or not. The factor of eight is the max, with any number or fraction less than that being an even better deal.

Zillow, Trulia, Redfin and other listing sites usually include a "rent" number in the property listings. Be aware that this may or may not reflect active rentals in the area, as it's an automatic calculation. Do your own homework in the classifieds, online rental listing sites, and any other sources people use to look for rentals, just as you would for any other **ARV**.

If you see a **"For Lease"** or **"For Rent"** sign in the neighborhood of your wholesale house, look up the address in the county records and see who owns it. Then, look up the owner and see if they own other properties. It will be immediately apparent if they own a number of properties, probably all rentals. They may be glad to hear about another wholesale rental prospect available at a favorable price!

Wholesaling specifically to rental investors can lead to even more profits for you than selling to the fix and flip investor. Don't overlook selling to them. Just keep in mind that they have slightly different criteria than the fix and flipper.

Chapter 4

Tools Needed for Success

This chapter will discuss some of the tools that I use or my previous coaching students have used to find success in Wholesaling Real Estate. You will need a phone number service that provides you the ability to make calls outside of using your personal everyday phone number. I would advise against a Google Voice number as they have limited support and you could potentially lose your call logs and all texts related to that number. I've included a couple of services below as recommendations.

Phone Number Services

-CallFire

https://www.callfire.com

Vumber

www.vumber.com

Below is a company that you can use to send bulk emails. For example when you build your buyers list and you find a property that you want to market the contract for you can use an email service to send one email that can reach large numbers of people at once without jeopardizing anyone's privacy on the list.

Email Marketing/Landing Page Service

http://mailchimp.com/pricing/entrepreneur/

Next is your CRM, your CRM is basically your database where customer information is updated and stored. For example if you speak with John Smith today and he says he is interested in selling in 3 weeks after his daughter's wedding; then you will want to keep track of those important details so that you can have a scheduled time to call him back as well as make mention of his daughter's wedding to help establish rapport. Below is a great cost effective CRM.

Customer Relationship Management tool CRM

-Less Annoying CRM ($10 monthly)

https://www.lessannoyingcrm.com/Pricing

Chapter 5

Practicing the Script

The important thing you want to understand about a script is that you will not need it soon. What do I mean by that? Well what I mean is the script should only be used as a guide to helping you extract the information from the seller that you are looking for. Practicing the script will be a necessary piece of your Wholesaling business so be sure to take it seriously and learn it as soon as possible so that you can make it yours. Below I have provided an example of a cold calling script that was shared with me that you would use when you are reaching out to a potential motivated seller out of the blue.

Cold Calling Script

Hello, I am looking for (First Name Only) This is (Your First Name) I know this call is out of the blue but.... I was calling about a property I believe you own on (Address)I just wanted to see if you would consider an offer on your property there? If "Yes", or "How much will you give me?" answer: Ok Great! Well... we purchase properties cash...

we pay all the closing costs...there are no real estate commissions... and the best part is we buy them completely as-is so you don't have to put another cent into the property...so...for an offer like that...how much would you take?(Check on Zillow) It looks like your home is about _______ sf is that right? Have you done any remodeling to the kitchen and bathrooms in the last 5 years?

(Option #1) We are buying homes similar to yours for around (66% of Zillow) _____________.

(Option #2) My partner runs all the numbers... so let me talk to him and call you back really soon.

(Option #3) The condition of the home is terrible or their motivation is high... get the appointment immediately! "I am in the area today do you mind if I swing by and take a look?

"If "No": I completely understand... do you have any other properties you would consider selling... maybe something that needs to be fully remodeled (or something that needs a little love)?

If "Yes/maybe in the future": Ok, great... should I call you back in a month? I am really looking for something that needs some love... have you done any major remodeling to the kitchen and bathrooms in the last 5 years? (this will open the conversation up for more "conditions of the home" questions)

Please save my name under (Your name) and Home Buyer in your phone in case anything changes.

Chapter 6

Documents Needed to Wholesale Real Estate

This chapter will be very brief as the documents that you will need to Wholesale a Real Estate deal will be better found by contacting a local attorney or a local Wholesaler. The documents you will need will be a (Standard Purchase and Sale Agreement also known as an "A-B") Once you have located a Cash buyer to sell your deal to you have them sign what's called (The Assignment Agreement also known as the "B-C").

You are Half Way There

You've come this far, so keep going!

What are Motivated Sellers and How to Find Them?

I usually try to stack my list when I, when I look for things, I try to combine things like maybe a distressed property code violation, tax lien and vacant. What I mean when I say vacant is no one's living in the property. It's just sitting there boarded up windows. Potentially grass has grown out of control, there is mail sticking out the mailbox etc. I mean, those are some great indications that that property is vacant. And think about it from this perspective, guys. If you owned a property and it was just sitting there vacant but you were still responsible for taxes,

Motivated Sellers

Some sellers are not in default, but they need to sell quickly for what they can get. Either the property or the seller's personal life has a problem that has the clock ticking on getting out of this property. People dealing with divorce, credit and financial problems, business problems, family problems, aging or illness all may be ready to accept a low offer with a fast closing. Think about what homeowners were up against when Covid-19 hit our nations. We never want to create the motivation; we only want to discover it. It may be a welcome relief to have an offer that requires nothing more of them than signing the papers and picking up the check as soon at closing. Look for ads with phrases asking for a fast sale or warning of a house needing work such as "need to sell fast", "fixer-upper", "handyman special", etc. Listing websites, internet searches, Facebook Marketplace, newspaper classifieds, and various online and print publications dealing with real estate in your area are places to find such ads. Some motivated sellers are actually real estate investors advertising their own wholesaling deals. Word of mouth tips, having an ear to the ground, developing personal contacts, and networking may yield an opportunity to save a worried homeowner the cost and bother of listing their problem property.

Direct Marketing

Direct marketing is where you find targeted lists to contact. For example using the websites provided in Chapter 4 you can create list to cold call or text blast. Those lists could include criteria such as (vacant properties, high equity, tax delinquent etc.) When you have a specified list to market to you then reach out to sellers of properties and track the responses in your database as the database will feed you your future deals. Remember just because someone does not want to sell now does not mean they will not want to sell in the future.

24

Chapter 9

Analyzing the Deal

Below I'm going to share a tool that I use in my business each and every day called Propstream. Propstream allows me to quickly analyze a deal and get accurate comparables to help me determine a maximum allowable offer "MAO" to my seller as well as determine what would be a good asking price to your cash buyers. This tool allows you to see the true owner's name as well as if there are any current tax liens on the property and even show you the entire purchase history of the property.

Propstream is the #1 tool my students and myself use to analyze deals and find important data on properties.

This is a must have for any Real Estate Investor regardless if you are seasoned or just getting started! Use the link below for a 7 day FREE TRIAL and DISCOUNT!

https://trial.propstreampro.com/nvip

Chapter 10

Making Offers and the Profit Factor

The Profit Factor

Now we have arrived at the good part! How much can you make on your deal …

You are calculating two profits: yours and that of your cash buyer, the person who will do the job of fixing the house and selling it to a future homebuyer or renting it out.

The investor's profit

A rule of thumb is to make your cash buyers profit at least twice as much as your wholesaling profit. He or she gets the greater share because they are taking on all the costs and risks of fixing the property, carrying it until it sells, and selling it to a homebuyer.

Your cash buyers often look for a profit as a percentage of their purchase price or even their expected combined costs to purchase, fix, carry, and sell the property – for example, 10% of their purchase price. Some cash buyers do want to earn simple minimum flat dollar amount such as $10,000 or more before they are willing to go ahead with a project. Each investor has their own idea of what makes a project worth a great deal. Talk to your cash buyers and get to know their expectations.

Your profit

Again, we're going to let the cash buyer take at least twice as much as you earn on your wholesale deal.

That said, you should have some standards of your own as to what your minimums are to make all of this worth your time and effort! Keep in mind your own costs of marketing, buying lists, finding and selling these wholesale properties and your most valuable cost of all, your time.

I would recommend as you start out that your profit should be $5,000. This is not a end goal number, but one that is a great place to start. As you get better at evaluating the properties and knowing what the cash buyer community will pay for particular deal types, you may be willing to make less or more depending on circumstances.

Your Purchase Price Offer

How much should you offer?

The Adventures In Wholesaling Street Academy rules for purchase prices for wholesalers:

• *Pay only up to 65% of the **ARV**.*

*• Sell to the investor for up to about 70% of the **ARV**.*

It is ALL about the purchase price

You've assessed the **ARV** as well as the rehab and selling costs. You know what your cash buyer expects to make for a profit, and you are awarding yourself an amount that is half of that. You are ready to figure out what you can offer the seller.

PRICE is the number one factor of what makes a deal. Without the right purchase price, there won't be enough profits for you. But, getting the house at the right price can overcome many less-than-ideal characteristics like bad location, difficult house configuration, etc.

Evaluation % of ARV Example

ARV (After-Repair Value) or Move-In Ready

Market Value -- **$150,000**

Less: Estimated Rehab Costs -- -**$17,000**

Less: Est. Interest for Six-Month Project **12% annual -$8,000**

Less: Estimated Selling Costs **7.5% -$11,250**

Less: Investor's Profit (flexible %) -- -**$10,000**

Less: Your Profit (flexible %) -- -**$5,000**

AX. PURCHASE PRICE To Contract with the Seller **$98,750 / 65%** of the **ARV**

ASSIGNMENT OR SALES PRICE

You sell to the real estate investor ...**$103,750** = 70% of the ARV

The investor's costs, itemized above +**$36,250**

INVESTOR'S TOTAL SPEND **$140,000**

If the sale to the home buyer is at **ARV** or above,

INVESTOR'S PROFIT is this or more ...**$10,000**

YOUR PROFIT

Less: Your marketing expenses to find sellers - **$750**

Less: Your expenses to find an investor buyer - **$500**

YOUR NET PROFIT **$3750**

Be ready to pass on the deal without purchasing if the seller won't agree to your price.

It is a numbers game so the more offers you make, the more deals you'll be closing on a consistent basis. The more deals you do, the more Home Runs you will have to make up for the properties you didn't get and struck out.

Chapter 11

Tips to Remember When Negotiating with the Seller

Remember that you can't give up your profit, because you can't afford to spend your valuable time underwriting other people's lives – either the seller's or the cash buyer's.

Do you need to have the inspection and estimate (or bid) before making an offer to purchase the property? This is a great question, because you should always assume that time is critical and you should get this seller's house under contract fast before another wholesaler or flipper finds this property or the seller gets cold feet.

The more experience you have with rehab costs, the more confidently you can calculate a generous allowance for the cost and go ahead with a purchase offer. HOWEVER DO NOT TRY TO BECOME AN EXPERT WITH REHAB COSTS! I say this because all you need is a general idea as the cash buyer will ultimately determine what the rehab cost for the project will be.

That being said, you do not need to have a formal estimate before making your offer to a motivated seller. In fact, I would recommend that you do NOT wait on making your offer due to the reasons stated above. TAKE ACTION!

But Shaun, how do you protect yourself from getting caught or even stuck with an expensive mistake if the cash buyers you approach know this rehab will cost more than you expected?

Get out your highlighter ... this is one of the most important tips in this book...

The purchase contract that you will use sets you up with an "out" clause during a pre-arranged inspection period. It is during this time that you will get the written estimate as well as secure your cash buyer.

If you find out that the property has more defects than you accounted for in your offer price, you can go back and renegotiate with the seller or simply back out of the deal. No harm, no foul. The estimate can also be a good negotiating tool with the seller if you need to renegotiate a lower price. Just remember to use the less than 65% of ARV formula on your initial offer and you should be in pretty good shape. This is yet another reason why getting the correct ARV is so critical to wholesaling.

Timing your offer for acceptance

You've found out as much as you possibly can about the seller and their motivations to sell.

What is pressuring them? How much time do they have? Especially dig deep for key dates the seller must meet.

If the seller claims they have no time pressures, find out how long they've been actively marketing the property. What are they paying in carrying costs – monthly mortgage payments, insurance, and ongoing upkeep? They may be ready to end the drama and the cash expenses after many months of trying to negotiate a sale without spending their own money on the fixes that home buyers demand.

If the seller didn't respond favorably the first time you negotiated, you want to be back on their doorstep immediately before the critical deadline with your solution to a need that – now, at least – matters more to them than the purchase price.

Circumstances change – sometimes rapidly, so be alert for your strategic timing opportunity.

• In one case in my own experience, a guy wanted to move quickly because he owned a home that was 8 months behind on the mortgage and was in risk of foreclosure. I was able to get his property under contract and assign my contract over to my end buyer who was more than happy to pay the 8 months that he was behind as he then said she would sell for what was owed on the mortgage which was little to nothing. So the seller wins; my end buyer wins and I win.

• Another cash buyer or wholesaler has a contract on the property, but it falls through when the buyer walks away. The sellers find their plans disrupted, and now they are facing having to re-list and more selling costs. Or they can accept your as-is cash offer, and move on. Keep an out our for when properties lose a sale contract, because that's good timing to present your offer (again, if you already tried once).

Every seller you speak with won't result in a deal. In fact, there's a good chance you'll be turned down more than you are successful at securing a contract at your needed price, especially when you are first starting.

That's why you have to keep plugging away, pushing forward and not compromising your own profits. Think about it; once the deal is done, your share has to pay for your time and expenses on all of the duds as well as the successful deals.

Just remember to keep on keeping on! The more sellers you can negotiate with and make offers to, the more deals that you are likely to get under contract.

How to find Cash Buyers for Your Deals

You should FOCUS 80% OF YOUR EFFORTS ON BUILDING A BUYERS LIST! And then REVERSE WHOLESALE!

REVERSE WHOLESALE STEPS!

Step 1. Interview your clients (BUYERS), build relationships and develop rapport with your CASH BUYERS in your market who have deep pockets; people spending money currently.

Step 2. Identify the inventory that your clients (BUYERS) are looking for specifically, spend time getting exact details on what they are looking for and what areas of town they are looking in. THIS INFORMATION IS EXTREMELY VALUABLE!

Step 3. Locate inventory that clients (BUYERS) desire

Step 4. Connect your SELLER to your BUYER with your signed agreements

Step 5. Close on the SALE!

Finding buyers is pretty simple. You can start to build your buyers list on a budget by posted what's called "Ghost Ads" on Craigslist or Facebook Marketplace with a headline that reads "Landlords Dream", or similar title. "Ghost Ads" are ads that you post that advertise an imaginary property in the area of town you are looking for buyers. Posting this ad will have hungry cash buyers reaching out to you for more details. When they do you can add them to your buyers list.

Ad example: 3bed 2bath near Downtown Atlanta must sell fast please call number on this ad for more details.

I usually do not put the full address, just the street name, city and state. This will generate interest and get the person viewing the ad to call you.

Bandit signs are another good way to attract buyers, (Check with your city or other local investors to see if this is ok in your area) Put about 30 of them out after 5pm on a Friday. You can buy these signs yourself from Home Depot, Hobby Lobby etc. Purchase signs that are 18x24 and corrugated.

KNOWING WHAT EACH BUYER IS WORTH TO YOU

Average Wholesale Deal to you is worth $10,000

Average number of purchases made by CASH BUYERS per year = 2.5

Average CASH BUYER annual Revenue = $25,000

$100,000 Annual Revenue = 4 CASH BUYERS

YOUR ARE 4 RELATIONSHIPS AWAY FROM $100,000 ANNUAL REVENUE WITH 4 CASH BUYERS!

Is your buyer a Landlord or Rehabber?

Typically, you are going to be selling to an investor who will either be a landlord or a rehabber. If the house is in an area where it's more rentals, most likely you will be selling to a landlord. If the area is more of a middle-lower high-class area, you will more than likely sell to a rehabber.

Chapter 13

Using a Closing Attorney or Title Company

Closing Procedures

Goal: To have every transaction handled quickly and smoothly, reducing the chances of further negotiations from buyer and/or seller and loss of a deal.

- The Title Company or Closing Attorney must be familiar with Double Closing, Assigning Contracts and working with investors. Find a couple to have on stand-by.

- Buyer pays all closing costs on both sides of the transaction, including mobile notary (except proration of taxes and anything against title) when assigning.

- A Buyer may not close with their own title company or closing attorney, however they are welcome to have their preferred title company or closing attorney review the closing documents at their own cost.

- The moment a deal is put under a Purchase Agreement and is submitted to you, please begin title preparations for a fast closing. What to say to Title Companies or Closing Attorney to not be charged for every search if the deal falls through for whatever reason. "Occasionally we will put a property under contract and it will not close, in order to not be charged for title work on these properties our team will close all of our houses and land deals through your title company or closing attorney."

- Seller will either close in person or via mobile notary; fee will be placed on HUD and paid for by Buyer at closing.

- Buyer is requested to wire funds 24 to 48 hours prior to closing

- If there is an agent in the deal their commission must be on the HUD and the Assignment Agreement. We absolutely never pay an agent outside of closing.

Chapter 14

Closing The Deal

3 STEPS TO CLOSING THE DEAL

1-PURCHASE CONTRACT WITH SELLER $50,000

2-ASSIGNMENT CONTRACT WITH BUYER $60,000

3-CLOSING AGENT CLOSES THE DEAL

Seller gets $50,000 - You get $10,000

Wash, Rinse, and Repeat!

You made it to the end of my book on Wholesaling Real Estate and you know what they say "most people never finish what they start." But that's not you this book should have helped you develop a winning mindset, help establish a strong purpose or WHY and gave you some useful information to help you take control of your financial future and start seeing success! Now go out there and get some deals closed!

About the Author

I started investing into Real Estate around 2016 after being laid off from a six figure sales executive job; sounds fancy and secure right? Well neither my title nor my hard work or my long hours of dedication and exceptional performance prevented me or my peers from getting that "we no longer need your services" notice that all employees dread. Never again would I allow myself to be in the position where I could be FIRED! That's when I found wholesaling. I have always had an entrepreneurial spirit and heard that Real Estate Investing could be a great, if not the best way, to secure financial freedom! Real Estate allows me to be a problem solver and a solution for the home owners and cash buyers that I assist through my Real Estate business. When I'm not involved with finding great off market deals or coaching, I do a lot of reading to stay in the know and to keep my skills sharp and mindset in check, I practice martial arts and enjoy working out at least 3 days a week, I love outdoor activities, hiking, live concerts, comedy shows, traveling and spending as much time as possible with my friends, family and children doing the things that we love.

When I think about new investors, I think analysis paralysis is one of the biggest issues holding you back! Too many think they need to know all there is to know before taking action. In my opinion, you have to be willing to take action daily, though it may be imperfect, you will see results! THE TIME IS NOW

Real Estate has Been a Game Changer!

That's why I created this book. To Give Back!

To allow people just like yourself, to create the life you've always dreamed of!

No More Waiting to be hired onto a job! No 9-5 Job Period! No 4 Years of College needed! No $100,000 in Debt! Absolutely Nothing Stopping You!

Help Me Help You Help Us All!

Shaun Young

Ceepreme